Made in the USA
Middletown, DE
25 July 2025

11248493R00057